"*The essence of the Yankees is that they win ... And that's why the history of the New York Yankees is virtually the history of baseball.*"

—Dave Anderson,
The New York Times

101 REASONS TO LOVE THE YANKEES

Ron Green, Jr.

Stewart, Tabori & Chang
New York

Introduction

It has been more than four decades since I was a seven-year old growing up in Charlotte, North Carolina, a nice southern town that had no idea it would one day be home to its own major league sports franchises with their own heroes, heartbreaks, and allegiances. Despite the years, I can still remember sitting in the barber's chair one Saturday afternoon, wishing I had the kind of hair that would allow me to wear a flat top while also thinking how lucky I was that my age matched Mickey Mantle's uniform number.

The Mick was on a flickering black and white television that afternoon and happened to hit a home run, and it was hard to find anything wrong with the world. That's an example of how the New York Yankees touched my generation, just as they touched generations before and after. They were not just New York's team, they were — to borrow a hackneyed phrase — America's first team. You didn't have to be from New York to love the Yankees. And you still don't.

I should have been a Minnesota Twins fan because their Class AA farm team was based in Charlotte and I spent dozens of summer nights at the old Griffith Park, watching Tony Oliva and others pass through on their way to the majors. But I loved the Yankees, largely because of Mantle, but not solely because of him. There were so many reasons — from the Babe to Lou Gehrig to Joe DiMaggio and beyond. And, of course, they won.

They still do. And they don't just win games and world championships. They win summer nights and the dreams of kids and grown-ups everywhere who imagine roaming center field in Yankee Stadium just like Mantle used to do.

Red Ruffing, Joe Gordon,
Bill Dickey, Charles Keller, and Joe DiMaggio

2 The Highlanders

Before they were the Yankees, they were the Highlanders. For 11 seasons beginning in 1903, the Highlanders played their games in Hilltop Park, which held approximately 15,000 fans. It all began when American League president Ban Johnson decided to move an existing team from Baltimore to compete with the New York Giants. Frank Farrell and Bill Deveney were the original owners and they paid $18,000 for the franchise, which drew its name from its ballpark.

3 Jack Chesbro

Chesbro was known as "Happy Jack," the nickname that's on his plaque in the Baseball Hall of Fame. One of the finest pitchers of his era, Chesbro was known for his spitball, which frustrated hitters for years as it dipped and darted near the plate. Chesbro owns the distinction of pitching the first game in Yankees history on April 20, 1903, but his legacy is one of extended success and one remarkable season. From 1901–06, Chesbro won 154 games and three times led the American League in winning percentage. It was his 1904 season that may remain unmatched. In that season, Chesbro won 41 games, completed 48 of the 51 games he started, and pitched 455 innings.

Jack Chesbro

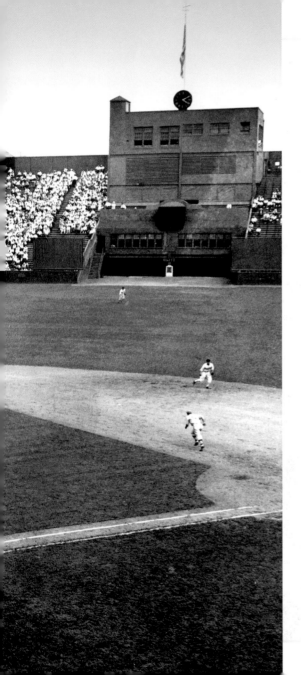

4 The Polo Grounds

Among the great stadiums in baseball history, few evoke as many wistful memories as the Polo Grounds. It was the home of three different teams over a span of more than 50 years, including a relatively brief time as the home of the Yankees. When the Highlanders moved to the Polo Grounds in 1913, they changed their name to the Yankees. They shared the park with the New York Giants and with its short left- and right-field lines, it was a dream park for Babe Ruth. The right-field line was only 258 feet deep while it was 277 feet to the left-field foul pole. Center field, however, was a canyon, the wall 455 feet from the plate. When the Yankees began out-drawing the Giants in the stadium they shared, Giants owner John McGraw decided he'd had enough. He evicted the Yankees after the 1922 season and they moved on — to their own place called Yankee Stadium.

5 Babe Ruth

Even now, nearly 70 years since he played his last game, Babe Ruth remains the most famous name in baseball history. He dominated a team, baseball, and the Golden Age of sports in America with his oversized personality and style. He was the player everyone wanted to see.

Baseball changed because of Ruth. Though he was an effective pitcher — helping the Boston Red Sox win the 1916 and 1918 World Series — Ruth became a home run hitter when he came to the Yankees in 1920. From then on, baseball — and the Yankees — were never the same.

6 The Babe's Numbers

- 714 home runs
- 2,211 runs batted in
- The first player to hit 30, 40, 50, and 60 home runs in a season
- .342 career batting average
- Averaged 50 home runs, 155 RBI and a .354 batting average from 1926 to 1931

7 The Curse of the Bambino

It was the stuff of legend or witchcraft or skullduggery. It inspired plays and songs and stories. There are those who will tell you it was the single most important event in baseball history and there are others who will tell you it was just a coincidence. But if there is any question why the Yankees–Red Sox rivalry may be the most intense in sports, it's not so much of what happened in December 1919, but what happened — or didn't happen — after that.

It was on December 26, 1919 that Boston owner Harry Frazee agreed to sell Babe Ruth to the Yankees for $125,000 and a $300,000 loan. At the time, the Red Sox had won five of the 15 World Series played, four of them with Babe Ruth on their team. The Yankees had not won a World Series. Since that day, any member of Red Sox Nation can tell you Boston went 86 long years between World Series titles. The Yankees, meanwhile, have won 26 through 2004.

8 Bobby Veach

He pinch-hit for Babe Ruth on August 9, 1925, the only time the Babe ever had a pinch-hitter.

9 Yankee Stadium

Considered the most famous stadium in the world, Yankee Stadium sits on a 10-acre site in the Bronx that cost $675,000 when it was purchased. Situated between 157th and 161st Streets, Yankee Stadium opened April 18, 1923, having cost $2.5 million to build and it came to be known as "The House That Ruth Built." The remodeled Yankee Stadium reopened in 1976 (after the Yankees spent two seasons playing in Shea Stadium) and remains one of the most recognizable structures in the world. Prize fights, football, soccer, and papal visits have also been held in Yankee Stadium.

"When you go to other parks, they hang banners for the wild-card or Eastern Division or Western Division champions. Around here, they don't hang anything unless its for being world champions."

—Chili Davis

10 The Facade

When the original Yankee Stadium opened, its roofline was encircled by a copper art deco frieze facade that became one of its most recognizable features. Through the years, Babe Ruth, Lou Gehrig, Joe DiMaggio, and Mickey Mantle played under the facade. Painted white in 1967 because it had begun to turn green, the facade was removed when the stadium was remodeled in 1976. A replica of the old facade was placed along a 550-foot stretch above the center-field bleachers.

19

11 The Number 4 Train

On its run from Crown Heights in Brooklyn, to Van Cortlandt Park in the Bronx, the number 4 train makes a stop beyond the right-field wall in Yankee Stadium. The elevated tracks are as much a part of the place as pinstripes and the facade.

Whitey Ford and Mickey Mantle

12 The Bat

Located near the front of Yankee Stadium, the 120-foot-high bat is actually a boiler stack painted to resemble a Louisville Slugger. With Babe Ruth's signature on it, the bat is a favorite spot for fans to have their photo taken.

13 The Short Porch

The right-field bleachers in Yankee Stadium have always tempted left-handed hitters. When the stadium originally opened, the right-field foul pole was only 296 feet from home plate. It has since been lengthened to 314 feet.

"I swing big, with everything I've got. I hit big or I miss big."

—Babe Ruth

Joe DiMaggio batting

Miller Huggins

14 Miller Huggins

He was known as the "Mighty Mite" because at only 5 feet, 6 inches tall, Huggins was a feisty man who wasn't afraid of anyone. A second baseman for 13 seasons in the majors, Huggins came to New York after a stint as player-manager for the St. Louis Cardinals. He managed the Yankees from 1918 through 1929 and led them to six pennants in an eight-year stretch. It was Huggins who managed the Yankees to their first three World Series titles. His enduring place in history is as the manager of the 1927 Yankees — the Murderer's Row team — which was built around Babe Ruth and Lou Gehrig.

15 Wally Pipp

He was the Yankees' starting first baseman until he was hit in the head by a pitch during batting practice on June 2, 1925. He was replaced in the starting lineup by Lou Gehrig, who played the next 2,130 games there. Pipp's decision to take the day off due to a lingering headache led him to joke that he took "the most expensive aspirin in history." The ultimate irony? It was Pipp, scouting for Indianapolis, who discovered Lou Gehrig and urged he be signed to a baseball contract.

16 Lou Gehrig

Known as the "Iron Horse," Gehrig played a record 2,130 consecutive games (surpassed by Cal Ripken, Jr. in 1995) while becoming one of the most famous and admired players in baseball history. His achievements were extraordinary:

– 493 home runs
– .340 career batting average
– 13 straight seasons with at least 100 RBI, including 184 in 1931
– .632 career slugging percentage
– 1,900 career RBI (third all time)

No wonder he's still known as the "Pride of the Yankees."

"He just went out and did his job every day."

—Bill Dickey

1927 Yankees

17 Murderer's Row

The heart of the lineup for the 1927 Yankees included Earle Combs, Tony Lazzeri, Babe Ruth, Lou Gehrig, and Bob Meusel.

18 Stealing Home

Babe Ruth did it 10 times. Lou Gehrig did it 15 times.

"The way a team plays as a whole determines its success. You may have the greatest bunch of individual stars in the world, but if they don't play together, the club won't be worth a dime."

—Babe Ruth

19 *Pride of the Yankees*

Gary Cooper played Lou Gehrig—and earned an Academy Award nomination—in the 1942 movie about the Yankees first baseman.

20 *The Babe*

John Goodman played the bigger-than-life role of Babe Ruth in 1991. It was an improvement on William Bendix's portrayal of the Babe years earlier.

21 *Damn Yankees*

The Yankees were so big in the 1950s they were a smash on Broadway, too. Gwen Verdon made famous the role of Lola in the play that ran for more than 1,000 performances on Broadway.

22 *That Touch of Mink*

The cast of this 1962 release included Cary Grant, Doris Day, Mickey Mantle, Roger Maris, and Yogi Berra.

The cast of *That Touch of Mink,* from left, Mickey Mantle, Doris Day, Cary Grant, Roger Maris, and Yogi Berra

Babe Ruth, Gary Cooper, and Bill Dickey on the set of *Pride of the Yankees*

Lou Gehrig crosses homeplate as Babe Ruth (no. 3) trots back to the dugout

23 Gehrig's Four-Homer Day

On June 3, 1932, the Yankees first baseman hit four home runs at Shibe Park in Philadelphia. In his fifth and final at bat, Gehrig's long fly ball to deep center field was caught inches from the fence.

24 Babe Ruth's Called Shot

In the fifth inning of the 1932 World Series, Ruth was facing Cubs' right-hander Charlie Root when, with two strikes, he stepped out of the batter's box. Legend has it Ruth pointed to the center-field bleachers. Others say he pointed to right field. Still others contend he never pointed at anything. Regardless, Ruth delivered a 436-foot home run to right-center field, his 15th and final World Series home run.

"I'm not a headline guy. I know that as long as I was following Ruth to the plate I could have stood on my head and no one would have known the difference."

—Lou Gehrig

25 The Logo

The interlocking "NY" is instantly recognizable around the world but, amazingly, Babe Ruth never wore it on his uniform. During Ruth's career, it had been removed from the uniform only to be reinstated in 1936 after Ruth had retired.

Lou Gehrig and Babe Ruth

26 Lou Gehrig's Farewell

On July 4, 1939, Gehrig—dying from amyotrophic lateral sclerosis—said this to the Yankee Stadium crowd gathered to honor him:

"Fans, for the past two weeks you have been reading about the bad break I got. Yet today I consider myself the luckiest man on the face of the earth. I have been in ballparks for 17 years and have never received anything but kindness and encouragement from you fans."

Less than two years later—exactly 16 years to the day that he replaced Wally Pipp at first base—the 37-year-old Gehrig died.

27 Joe McCarthy

Although he never played in the majors, McCarthy earned a place in the Hall of Fame for his work as a manager. McCarthy had a stern, business-like approach and the bottom line told his story. In 16 seasons with the Yankees (1931–46), McCarthy's teams won 62 percent of their games and, starting in 1936, won four straight World Series titles.

28 Frank Crosetti

For 37 seasons, Crosetti wore a Yankees uniform. He spent 17 seasons as the short-stop, winning eight World Series in the process, and then he became the team's third-base coach for another 20 years. When Crosetti finally retired, he had participated in 24 World Series as a member of the Yankees.

Joe McCarthy

Third-base coach Frank Crosetti congratulates
Mickey Mantle after Mantle's home run

Red Ruffing

29 Red Ruffing

Ruffing was one of the Yankees' all-time great pitchers, going 231–124 during his New York career. He was part of seven championship teams and was good enough at the plate that he batted better than .300 eight times.

30 Lefty Gomez

This may say it all about Gomez's career in pinstripes — he had a 6–0 record in the World Series, a major league record. He was part of five World Series champions and became the second Hispanic player inducted into the Baseball Hall of Fame.

"The secret of my success was clean living and a fast outfield."

—Lefty Gomez

Lefty Gomez

Bill Dickey

31 Bill Dickey

If the subject is catchers, Dickey's name belongs in the discussion. He was the consummate man behind the plate. With an innate understanding of pitchers, Dickey knew how to manage games and he was capable of making an impact on them with both his glove and his bat. His .362 batting average in 1936 remains the highest single-season average for a catcher in history.

32 No. 8

The uniform number worn by Yankee catchers Yogi Berra and Bill Dickey. It was retired twice, in honor of each of them.

"I loved to make a great defensive play. I'd rather do that than hit a home run."

—Bill Dickey

"*It ain't over till it's over.*"

—Yogi Berra

33 Yogi Berra

No player in baseball history has won more world championships than Berra, who won 10. Throw in 14 pennants, 15 All-Star Game appearances, a perfect fielding record in 1958, a place in the Baseball Hall of Fame, three MVP awards and a spot in the hearts of baseball fans everywhere and it's easy to see why there's never been anyone like Yogi.

34 Yogi-isms

"When you come to a fork in the road, take it."

"You can observe a lot by watching."

"It's déjà vu all over again."

"It gets late early out here."

Roger Maris, Yogi Berra, and Mickey Mantle

35 Monument Park

The history of the great Yankees is honored in the small park located between the bullpens in the Yankee Stadium outfield. It's there that the most famous Yankees are remembered for their contributions with plaques and monuments. In many ways, it's a history of the game. Babe Ruth. Lou Gehrig. Joe DiMaggio. Mickey Mantle— they're each honored there, and so are others whose legacy is part of what has made the Yankee dynasty what it is. Fans arriving early to games can tour the park and be reminded of the legends who helped create baseball's most successful franchise.

"Playing eighteen years in Yankee Stadium for you folks was the best thing that could ever happen to a ball player."

—Mickey Mantle

36 Joe DiMaggio

DiMaggio was a classic in every way. In center field, he could run like the wind to make plays. At the plate, he was among the finest hitters of his or any generation. As a man, he was the consummate gentleman. He even married Marilyn Monroe. DiMaggio had an amazing grace about him.

"There was an aura about him. He walked like no one else walked. He did things so easily. He was immaculate in everything he did. Kings of state wanted to meet him and be with him."

—Phil Rizzuto

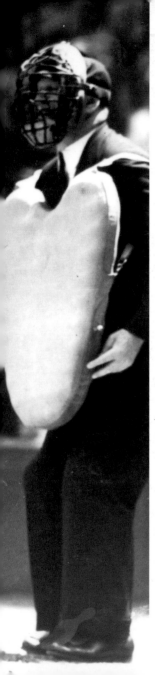

37 Joe DiMaggio's Hitting Streak

Of all the great Yankees records, none may be greater than Joe DiMaggio's 56-game hitting streak in 1941. From May 15 through July 17, DiMaggio had a base hit in every game he played, hitting .408 in the stretch.

And when it ended? DiMaggio went hitless one game — because Cleveland Indians third baseman Ken Keltner made two great plays to rob him of hits — then started another streak of 16 consecutive games with a base hit. Just as impressive was the 61-game hitting streak DiMaggio had as a minor leaguer.

38 The DiMaggio Record

Injuries and a stint in the military limited DiMaggio to only 13 seasons with the Yankees. Of all the numbers he accumulated, the one that mattered most to DiMaggio was this one: the Yankees won nine World Series in his 13 seasons.

"He was beyond question one of the greatest players of the century."

—Mickey Mantle

39 Mickey Owen's Dropped Third Strike

Trailing Brooklyn 4–3 in the fourth game of the 1941 World Series, the Yankees were down to their last strike when Dodgers' catcher Mickey Owen dropped the third strike on Tommy Heinrich, who reached first base. The Yankees scored four runs and won the game.

40 Casey Stengel

As great a character as the Yankees themselves, Stengel managed the Yankees through their greatest run, adding his own splash of color to the remarkable journey. Stengel was the Yankees manager from 1949 through 1960 and the numbers his teams accumulated were remarkable. They won 10 American League pennants and seven World Series, including five in a row starting in 1949.

"Most ball games are lost, not won."

—Casey Stengel

Casey Stengel

Mel Allen

41 Mel Allen

The voice of the Yankees through so many glory days.

42 Red Barber

A voice that wound up in the Baseball Hall of Fame.

43 Phil Rizzuto

"Holy Cow."

44 Robert Merrill

"Oh say can you see..."

53

Phil Rizzuto

45 Whitey Ford

Simply put, he was the greatest pitcher in Yankees history.
The left-hander spent 16 seasons with the Yankees, amassing
236 victories and a .690 winning percentage that remains
the best for any left-hander with at least 200 wins. He was
a master on the mound, helping the Yankees win seven
World Series in the 1950s and 1960s. During the midst of
the M&M Boys great home run chase in 1961, Ford quietly
put together a 25–4 record.

46 Legends Field

It starts each February in Florida at the same place—
Legends Field in Tampa. The spring training home of the
Yankees is a place full of possibilities where the playing
field has the same dimensions as Yankee Stadium.

*"You would be amazed how many important outs
you can get by working the count down to where
the hitter is sure you're going to throw to his
weakness, and then throw to his power instead."*

—Whitey Ford

Whitey Ford

Elston Howard

47 Elston Howard

Before he ever played a game for the Yankees, Elston Howard made history. He was the first African-American Yankee. Howard was a quiet man, but his performance on and off the field spoke volumes. He handled the challenges of integration with dignity and in 1963 he became the first African-American to win the American League's Most Valuable Player award.

48 The Farm System

Through the years, the Yankees have cultivated their talent through a system of minor league clubs that once numbered 24, though it is now down to six. While the modern-day Yankees have been active in the free-agent market, the farm system has remained the lifeblood of the franchise, producing Derek Jeter, Bernie Williams, Mariano Rivera, and Jorge Posada, among others. In the past, Lou Gehrig, Whitey Ford, and Mickey Mantle came up through the farm system.

"You know, I never would have gone through what Jackie Robinson went through. I don't think I could have taken it. I give Jackie a great deal of credit for opening the way up for me."

—Elston Howard

49 Mickey Mantle

A product of the heartland with a name made for a baseball hero, Mickey Mantle may have been the most beloved Yankee of all time. He was both superhuman and utterly human, a combination that endeared him to people who could see beyond the pinstripes and the number 7 to a man who captured the hearts of a generation.

Mantle's numbers were classic:
– 3 Most Valuable Player awards
– 16-time All-Star
– 10 seasons of hitting .300 or better
– 536 career home runs
– 18 World Series home runs

And Mantle himself was a Yankee classic.

"The only thing I can do is play baseball. I have to play ball. It's the only thing I know."

—Mickey Mantle

50 Mantle's Tape-Measure Home Run

Playing in Griffith Stadium in Washington, D.C., on April 17, 1953, Mantle connected for one of the most prodigious home runs of his career. He slugged a pitch over the left-field wall in the stadium, beyond the bleachers and across the street into a row of houses. The shot was later measured at 565 feet, helping create the mystique of the tape-measure home run.

51 Mantle's 1956 Season

Just entering the prime of his career, Mantle had a season for the ages when he won the Triple Crown while leading the Yankees to their 17th World Series title. Mantle hit .353, slammed 52 home runs, and drove in 130 runs, the most productive season in his career. No wonder, in his prime, Mantle was considered the most powerful hitter in the game, and the fastest.

"After a home run, I had a habit of running the bases with my head down. I figured the pitcher already felt bad enough without me showing him up rounding the bases."

—Mickey Mantle

52 Don Larsen's Perfect Game

On October 8, 1956, Larsen pitched Game 5 of the World Series for the Yankees against the Brooklyn Dodgers and retired all 27 batters he faced in order. It is the only perfect game ever thrown in the World Series.

Don Larsen

53 Roger Maris

There was more to Roger Maris than his 61 home runs in 1961. Playing in the same outfield with Mickey Mantle — one half of the M&M Boys — Maris was a strong left-handed hitter who was also an excellent right fielder. He never liked the attention and pressure that came with his pursuit of Babe Ruth's record and it took its toll on Maris. But he endured, as has his place in history.

"I never wanted all this hoopla. All I wanted is to be a good ballplayer and hit 25 or 30 homers, drive in a hundred runs, hit .280 and help my club win pennants. I just wanted to be one of the guys, an average player having a good season."

—Roger Maris

54 The Great Home Run Chase

In 1961, Roger Maris and Mickey Mantle—teammates and good friends—chased Babe Ruth's single-season home run record. Back and forth they went until September when health problems forced Mantle to settle for 54 home runs. Maris kept going and the M&M Boys had a place in history, combining for 115 home runs.

55 No. 61

On October 1, 1961, Roger Maris hit a fourth-inning pitch from Boston pitcher Tracy Stallard into the right-field bleachers in Yankee Stadium—the sixth row of section 33 to be precise—and Babe Ruth's single-season home run record was broken—by another Yankee.

"I don't want to be Babe Ruth. He was a great ballplayer. I'm not trying to replace him. The record is there and damn right I want to break it, but that isn't replacing Babe Ruth."

—Roger Maris

Roger Maris and
Mickey Mantle

56 "Mrs. Robinson"

The Simon and Garfunkel song, from the movie *The Graduate*, included one of the most famous lines from the rock and roll era: "Where have you gone Joe DiMaggio, a nation turns its lonely eyes to you…"

57 *Ball Four*

Jim Bouton had left the Yankees by the time he penned *Ball Four*, one of the most famous sports books of all time. But Bouton's days with the Yankees were remembered in the tale of what baseball can be like from the inside.

58 Mike Kekich and Fritz Peterson

During spring training in 1973, the Yankee pitchers announced they had swapped their wives, their families, and their dogs.

"You spend a good piece of your life gripping a baseball and in the end it turns out that it was the other way around all the time."

—Jim Bouton

Chris Chambliss

59 The First Designated Hitter

The designation belongs to Ron Blomberg of the Yankees, who earned the distinction by going 1 for 3 against the Boston Red Sox on April 6, 1973.

60 Catfish Hunter

On New Year's Eve, 1974, Catfish Hunter helped ignite the free-agent era in baseball when he signed a five-year contract worth $3.75 million. The willingness of the Yankees to seek and sign the best free-agent talent on the market would become an integral part of the club's continued success.

61 Chris Chambliss' Home Run

It was the bottom of the ninth, with the score tied 6–6 in the deciding fifth game of the 1976 American League Championship Series between the Yankees and Kansas City Royals. Chambliss clubs the pitch from Mark Littell just over the right-field wall and the Yankees win the American League pennant for the 30th time.

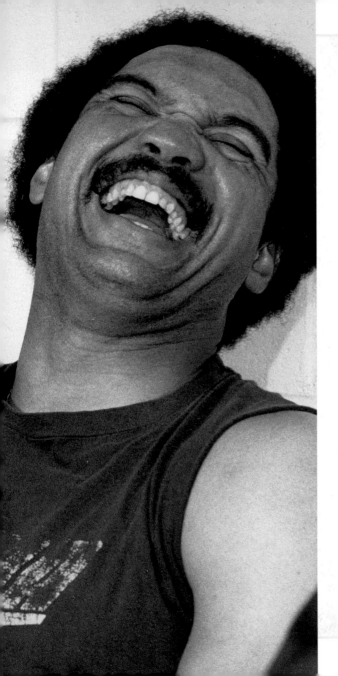

62 The Bronx Zoo

It was the perfect nickname for the franchise in the late 1970s. It seemed that every week another storm would erupt inside the Yankees locker room or in a New York tabloid. Controversy became the common denominator with the Yankees.

The Yankees were stuffed with over-sized egos and an abundance of talent. The stew created when Thurman Munson, Sparky Lyle, Reggie Jackson, Billly Martin and the others put on the pinstripes read like cheap fiction. They called each other names. They squabbled. They pouted. One Saturday afternoon, Martin and Jackson had to be pulled apart in the Yankee dugout when they went after each other. It was always something. Through it all, the Yankees won consecutive World Series in 1977 and 1978.

63 Billy Martin

He's hired. He's fired. He's hired. He's fired.

Owner George Steinbrener hired Martin to manage the Yankees five times and five times he fired him. It reached the point the two even made commercials poking fun at how often their relationship switched from hot to cold. Martin, classically tough and combative, managed the Yankees from 1975–78; again in 1979; again in 1983; again in 1985; and again in 1988. The result was two American League championships, the 1977 World Series, and a special place in the Yankees' history.

His frequent battles with Steinbrenner over-shadowed Martin's long contribution to the Yankees. He retired with a career .333 batting average in the World Series and his feisty style left its mark on the franchise. Despite his temper, Martin became a beloved Yankee and one of Mickey Mantle's closest friends.

64 Reggie Jackson

He called himself "the straw that stirs the drink" and Jackson's five seasons in pinstripes were high drama. Jackson had an ego the size of Manhattan but he also had an ability to rise to the occasion. He feuded with teammates and with manager Billy Martin, but Jackson found a way to deliver.

Jackson was never better than that October night when he hit three consecutive pitches out of the park in Game 6 of the 1977 World Series, securing a championship for the Yankees and his place in history.

65 The Reggie Bar

Reggie Jackson claimed he'd be so big in New York they'd name a candy bar after him—and he was right. When the bar was unveiled in 1978 teammate Catfish Hunter cracked, "Open it and it tells you how good it is." And Jackson showed it. In front of a sell-out crowd at Yankee Stadium on a day when everyone had been given a free Reggie Bar, Jackson smacked a 3-run homer to beat the Chicago White Sox.

66 "Reg-gie, Reg-gie!"

With the World Series on the line in Game 6 in 1977, Reggie Jackson hammered three home runs on three straight pitches off Los Angeles Dodgers pitchers, clinching the Yankees' first world championship in 15 years. In fact, Jackson hit four straight home runs, hitting one out in his final at bat in Game 5, forever securing his place as "Mr. October."

67 Sparky Lyle

He was a symbol of the 1970s with his handlebar mustache and devil-may-care attitude but when he was on the mound, Sparky Lyle knew how to put away baseball games. He became the first relief pitcher to win the Cy Young Award when he had 26 saves while helping the Yankees win the 1977 World Series, ending a 15-year drought between championships.

68 Thurman Munson

Munson was the essence of toughness. With his thick moustache and fierce game face, he was a ferocious competitor. In many ways, Munson was the heart and soul of the Yankee teams that won three straight American League titles (1976–78) and two World Series. Rookie of the year in 1970 and American League MVP in 1976,

Just the fifth captain in Yankees history, Munson's career was cut short after he was killed at age 32 when his plane crashed short of the runway at the Akron-Canton, Ohio, Regional Airport on August 2, 1979. Munson's locker remains empty in perpetuity.

"Thurman was indispensable and irreplaceable…"

—George Steinbrenner

69 Bucky Dent's Home Run

He hit 27 home runs in his career as a Yankee but only one is remembered. It came October 2, 1978, in the seventh inning of a one-game playoff at Boston's Fenway Park against Mike Torrez.

The Yankees should have already been finished. They trailed the Red Sox by 14 games in the American League East on July 19, but it was the Red Sox who had to win their last eight games to force a one-game playoff for the division title. The Yankees were down 2-0 when Dent came to the plate in the top of the seventh with two men on base. Dent had batted only .140 in his previous 20 games but he floated a 1-1 pitch over Fenway Park's Green Monster and sent Red Sox Nation into despair.

*"Bucky ****ing Dent."*

—Don Zimmer, Red Sox manager

Ron Guidry

70 Guidry Strikes Out 18 Angels

Ron Guidry set an American League record for left-handed pitchers when he struck out 18 California Angels on June 17, 1978. Guidry, nicknamed "Louisiana Lightning," was virtually unhittable, at one stretch striking out 12 of 13 batters.

71 25–3

In 1978, Ron Guidry had a season like few pitchers have ever had. He went 25–3 in the regular season with a 1.74 earned run average. He allowed just 187 hits in 273 2/3 innings, struck out 248 batters, and walked only 72, while throwing nine shutouts.

72 July 4, 1983

On America's birthday, Dave Righetti pitched the first no-hitter by a left-hander in Yankee Stadium history, shutting down the Boston Red Sox 4–0.

Dave Righetti

73 Graig Nettles

For 11 seasons, Nettles was the Yankees' rock at third base. He was an exceptional fielder, a consistent home run hitter, and a fiery personality who earned the rare honor of being named a Yankee captain.

74 Dave Winfield

He was a star before he joined the Yankees and when he signed a 10-year contract with the club as a free agent, Winfield became almost bigger than life in a city that loves its stars. Then he hit a game-winning home run in his first game as a Yankee. Though he feuded with owner George Steinbrenner at times, Winfield was an exceptional player who made his mark in the Bronx. That didn't stop Steinbrenner from occasionally calling him "Mr. May," a jab in reference to Reggie Jackson's "Mr. October" moniker.

"When I was a little boy, I wanted to be a baseball player and join the circus. With the Yankees, I have accomplished both."

—Graig Nettles

Dave Winfield

Goose Gossage

75 Goose Gossage

Big, bold, and full of bravado, Gossage was an intimidating presence on the mound. With a fastball whistling at nearly 100 miles per hour and just a hint of uncertainty about where it might go, Gossage kept opposing hitters on edge. In seven seasons with the Yankees, Gossage had a 2.14 earned run average and 151 saves.

76 The Pine Tar Incident

On July 24, 1983, Kansas City's George Brett thought he'd hit a two-out, two-run home run off Goose Gossage to give the Royals a 5–4 lead until Yankees manager Billy Martin pointed out to umpire Tim McClelland that the pine tar on the handle of Brett's bat was in violation of the rules. Brett exploded from the Royals' dugout when the home run was nullified and was immediately ejected from the game. The Yankees won 4–3 but American League president Lee McPhail later ordered the game to be resumed from the point following Brett's home run after deciding it should be allowed. The Royals ultimately won but Brett's reaction rushing from the Yankee Stadium dugout remains a part of baseball history.

77 Don Mattingly

He spent 14 seasons with the Yankees, usually playing first base, and he never won a World Series. In fact, he never played in one. But "Donnie Baseball" carved his own place in Yankees history with his understated style and his professionalism. He did it quietly and brilliantly.

78 The Nicknames

The Bronx Bombers. Donnie Baseball. Scooter. The Yankee Clipper. The Iron Horse. Murderer's Row. The Sultan of Swat. Mr. October. The Ole Perfessor. The Boss.

"I'm glad I don't have to face that guy every day. He has that look that few hitters have. I don't know if it's his stance, his eyes or what, but you can tell he means business."

—Dwight Gooden on Don Mattingly

Don Mattingly

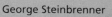
George Steinbrenner

79 George Steinbrenner

The owner of the New York Yankees since 1973, Steinbrenner has spent more than three decades as "The Boss." A shipbuilder by trade, Steinbrenner has been aggressive, egotistical, flamboyant, and bullish. He has been suspended and reinstated, cursed and cursed again. But he has always tried to keep the Yankees special, no matter the cost, no matter the situation. He is not just any owner, but the Yankees aren't just any franchise.

80 George Costanza

As the assistant traveling secretary for the Yankees in *Seinfeld*, George managed to mess up everything he touched. He tried to help Danny Tartabull fix his swing, proposed Jon Voight Day at the stadium, and purchased cotton uniforms for the Yankees, which shrunk after they were washed. Costanza introduced George Steinbrenner to calzones but even that backfired.

"Winning is the most important thing in my life, after breathing. Breathing first, winning next."

—George Steinbrenner

Joe Torre

81 Joe Torre

When the Yankees hired him before the 1996 season, the first question asked was "why?" Torre had been a good player and a solid manager but he hadn't done anything to suggest he would become a legend in pinstripes. With the perfect temperament for managing in the home dugout at Yankee Stadium, Torre made his team a fixture in the postseason, winning three straight World Series and four of five, starting in 1996.

"When we lost, I couldn't sleep at night. When we win, I can't sleep at night. But, when you win, you wake up feeling better."

—Joe Torre

82 Derek Jeter

Jeter became the face of a new generation of great Yankees teams, playing shortstop and winning championships. He joined the Yankees in 1996 and won four World Series rings in his first five seasons, piling up three 200-hit seasons in the process, all by the time he was 26 years old.

83 The Captains

There haven't been many. Hal Chase (1912); Roger Peckinpaugh (1914–21); Babe Ruth (1925); Everett Scott (1922–25); Lou Gehrig (1935–41); Thurman Munson (1976–79); Graig Nettles (1982–84); Willie Randolph (1986–88); Ron Guidry (1986–89); Don Mattingly (1991–95); Derek Jeter (2000–present).

"He'd been summoned by the baseball gods; to carry the torch, to help save the team and the stadium and maybe even the game of baseball itself."

—Peter Richmond on Derek Jeter, *GQ*

Derek Jeter

84 Jeff Maier

The 12-year-old Yankee fan caught Derek Jeter's fly ball at the fence in the first game of the 1996 ALCS when New York was trailing Baltimore 4–3 in the eighth. Umpires ruled it was a home run though replays showed it was not. The Yankees went on to win 5–4 in 11 innings.

Jeff Maier

85 Jim Leyritz's Home Run

Down 2 games to 1 to the Atlanta Braves in the 1996 World Series, and trailing 2–1 in the eighth inning of Game 4, Leyritz smashed a 3-run homer that helped the Yankees win the game and, ultimately, another championship.

Jim Leyritz

86 114 Wins

In 1998, the Yankees won 114 regular-season games, winning the American League East by 22 games. Add in their postseason victories over Texas, Cleveland, and San Diego and the Yankees went 125–50, arguably the greatest season ever.

87 David Wells' Perfect Game

On May 17, 1998, David Wells was perfect against the Minnesota Twins, winning a 4–0 decision while facing the minimum 27 batters in Yankee Stadium. Barely a year later, teammate David Cone would duplicate the feat against Montreal.

88 David Cone's Perfect Game

Don Larsen was there and so was Yogi Berra when Cone threw the 16th perfect game in history, beating the Montreal Expos 6–0 on July 19, 1999.

David Wells

David Cone

89 22–1

Playing in Fenway Park on June 19, 2000, the Yankees handed their bitter rival, the Boston Red Sox, a 22–1 defeat, their worst home loss ever.

Ted Williams, left, and Joe DiMaggio

90 The Red Sox Rivalry

By winning as often as they have, the Yankees have made themselves every team's rival. But there is nothing in baseball—and few like it in any sport—as passionate and enduring as the Yankees and Red Sox rivalry. From the sale of Babe Ruth through Bucky Dent, Aaron Boone, and on to Alex Rodriguez and the stunning 2004 ALCS, it continues in perpetuity, the flame forever burning.

Mariano Rivera

91 Mariano Rivera

From the mid-1990s and into the 21st century, Rivera entering the game was a chilling sight to opponents. With wicked control and a cold-blooded approach to his work, Rivera established himself as perhaps the greatest closer in history, doing most of his best work in the postseason.

92 "YMCA"

When the Yankee Stadium grounds crew comes out between innings to drag the infield during home games, it's a musical number. With the Village People's famous song "YMCA" playing in the stadium, the crew turns an ordinary task into a performance.

93 "New York, New York"

"Start spreading the news..."

"Without question we're talking about the best reliever, in my opinion, in the history of baseball. This guy has become branded with the Yankee logo. People are going to remember this man for so long for what he's done."

—Brian Cashman on Mariano Rivera

94 Roger Clemens

The owner of five Cy Young Awards when he joined the Yankees, Roger Clemens wanted what he didn't have — a world championship. He got two of those as a Yankee (1999 and 2000). He also won a sixth Cy Young Award and his 1-hit, 15-strikeout shutout of Seattle in the 2000 ALCS remains one of the best postseason pitching performances ever.

95 20–1

Roger Clemens became the first pitcher in major league history to post a 20–1 record, doing so with a victory over the Chicago White Sox on September 19, 2001.

"Everybody kind of perceives me as being angry. It's not anger, it's motivation."

—Roger Clemens

Roger Clemens

Mike Piazza, left, and Roger Clemens

96 The Subway Series

For a time, Subway Series were routine in New York City. Before 2000, there had been 13 of them, including seven in a 10-year stretch beginning in 1947. Ten times, the Yankees won the Subway Series, beating either the Dodgers or Giants in the process. Then, in 2000, the Yankees faced the Mets in a long-awaited renewal of the Subway Series. The city was captivated by the drama, especially when Roger Clemens and Mike Piazza went eye to eye in a classic pitcher-hitter duel. Ultimately, the Yankees won their third straight World Series, beating the Mets 4 games to 1.

97 The Derek Jeter Play

It was the kind of play that defines a career. Derek Jeter had already established himself as a Yankee legend, having arrived at shortstop at the start of a great post-season run, and he had shown the knack for making big plays when it mattered the most.

In Game 3 of the 2001 ALCS against the Oakland Athletics, the Yankees were leading 1-0 in the seventh inning when a base hit sent the A's Jeremy Giambi barreling toward home plate with the tying run. In the outfield, Shane Spencer hustled a throw in the general direction of the plate. As Giambi rushed toward the plate with a run that could swing the series, Jeter raced into foul territory to cut off Spencer's throw. With stunning imagination and quickness, Jeter backhanded the ball to catcher Jorge Posada, who laid the tag on Giambi to save the Yankee win.

Jorge Posada tags out Jeremy Giambi
as Derek Jeter looks on

98 Aaron Boone's Home Run

It was like Bucky Dent all over again.

This time, it was the bottom of the 11th inning in Game 7 of the ALCS against the Red Sox. All the passion and fire and history between the two franchises seemed to ride on every pitch, every hit, every out. The Red Sox had been five outs away from the World Series only to surrender three runs in the bottom of the eighth inning when Boston manager Grady Little decided to leave starting pitcher Pedro Martinez in the game, allowing New York to tie the game at 5 and force extra innings. In the bottom of the 11th, Boston sent out knuckleball ace Tim Wakefield to pitch in relief, looking for three more outs to get to the 12th inning. Wakefield threw one pitch and Boone—who had been acquired earlier in the season in a trade with the Cincinnati Reds—hit it over the left-field fence to give the Yankees their 39th American League pennant.

"In Boston fans are wailing,
and they're cursing at the moon,
For there is no joy in Beantown
thanks to Aaron Bleepin' Boone."

—John Roche, from www.ultimateyankees.com

Aaron Boone

99 The Alex Rodriguez Deal

For weeks, the Boston Red Sox tried to work a deal that would bring Alex Rodriguez, considered the game's best player, to Beantown. There were discussions and scenarios and possibilities fueling the off-season in Boston. Then nothing.

And then, not long before spring training began in 2004, the Yankees announced they had acquired A-Rod in a stunning deal that once again reminded everyone in baseball—particularly in Boston—that they're still the Yankees.

100 The Money

In 1949, the Yankees made Joe DiMaggio baseball's first $100,000 per season player.

In 2001, Derek Jeter's 10-year contract was worth $189,000,000.

"I'm pretty excited, this is a big, big one."

—George Steinbrenner, on the Alex Rodriguez trade

Alex Rodriguez

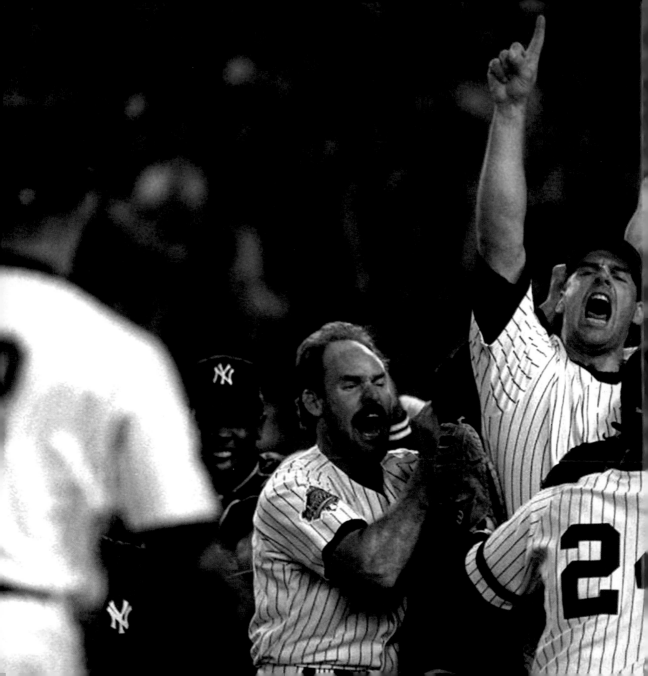

101

26 World Series Titles

And counting.

10 Reasons to Hate the Red Sox

Okay, so hate might be a strong word. Or maybe not strong enough. But at the very least, here are 10 reasons to really, really, really dislike the Red Sox. And this is just a start.

1 1919

The Red Sox waited until 1919 to sell Babe Ruth to the Yankees. Just think how many more World Series the Yankees would have won had the Babe joined them earlier.

2 Red Sox Nation

The fans have given themselves a nickname and take a certain amount of pleasure from their long suffering.

3 Monster Seats

They put seats on top of the Green Monster in Fenway Park.

4 Pedro Martinez

Martinez threw Yankees bench coach Don Zimmer to the ground. Okay, so Zimmer shouldn't have come charging like a bull at Pedro but, seriously, he's an old man. At least help him up.

5 "Yankees Suck" t-shirts

They're so annoying.

6 Ben Affleck

He has become the voice all things New England and the cleft-chinned face of Red Sox Nation.

7 Bill Buckner

The way Red Sox fans have treated Bill Buckner is disgraceful. Give it a rest. Even if he fielded the ball, the game was going to be tied. The Red Sox still may have blown it.

8 Nomar Garciaparra

The Red Sox traded Nomar Garciaparra. He was classy, gave them the best years of his career and, suddenly, they didn't need him any more. He deserved better treatment.

9 Ted Williams vs. Babe Ruth

The insufferable insistence of Red Sox fans that Ted Williams was the greatest hitter that ever lived. No, he wasn't. Babe Ruth was.

10 2004

The Red Sox completed the greatest comeback in baseball history on Mickey Mantle's birthday when they defeated the Yankees 10-3 in Game 7 of the ALCS after trailing three games to none, a feat never before achieved in the major leagues.

Acknowledgments

This must begin with a word of thanks to Beth Huseman, Leslie Stoker, Galen Smith and the good people at Stewart, Tabori & Chang, who understand the passion and magic of the New York Yankees. Their commitment to this project is greatly appreciated.

Also, thanks go to Mary Tiegreen, whose imagination led to the creation of this book and others like it. In her own way, she has earned her pinstripes.

Thanks to Stan Olson, who knows more about the Yankees than anyone should and who, after all these years, still gets the same charge from them he did as a kid.

A special thank you to my brother, Dave, who, despite being a Boston Red Sox fan, brought this all together.

To Kevin O'Sullivan at AP Wide World, and Bill Burdick and staff at the National Baseball Hall of Fame Library, thank you for all your time and effort.

Also, to my wife, Tamera, and daughter, Molly; my parents, Ron and Beth Green; my sister, Edie and all the McGlones, as well as the Macchias, you're better than the '27 Yankees.

Of course, no book on the Yankees would be complete without a thank you to Harry Frazee, the former Boston Red Sox owner, who decided it was a good idea to sell Babe Ruth to the Yankees in 1919.

Joe McCarthey

Photo Credits

Lou Gehrig and Joe DiMaggio

A Tiegreen Book

Text copyright © 2005 Ron Green, Jr.
Compilation copyright © 2005 Mary Tiegreen

Editor: Beth Huseman
Designer: David Green, Brightgreen Design
Production Manager: Jane Searle

Published in 2005 by
Stewart, Tabori & Chang
115 West 18th Street
New York, NY 10011
www.abramsbooks.com

Cataloging-in-Publication Data is on file
with the Library of Congress
101 Reasons to Love the Yankees
ISBN: 1-58479-401-1

101 Reasons to Love the Yankees is a book in the
101 REASONS TO LOVE™ Series.

101 REASONS TO LOVE™ is a trademark of
Mary Tiegreen and Hubert Pedroli.

The text of this book was composed in ITC Giovanni,
ITC New Baskerville, ITC Cheltenham, and Frutiger.

Printed in China

10 9 8 7 6 5 4

Stewart, Tabori & Chang is a subsidiary of

LA MARTINIÈRE
GROUPE